preMEDITATED

an activity book for true crime fanatics who want
to kill time and survive boredom

daily exercises which are not
all that relaxing, meditative,
or good for mental health...

ISBN-13: 978-1975778927

For my friends, who know how weird I am
and accept me anyway - or at least have
yet to report me to the authorities.

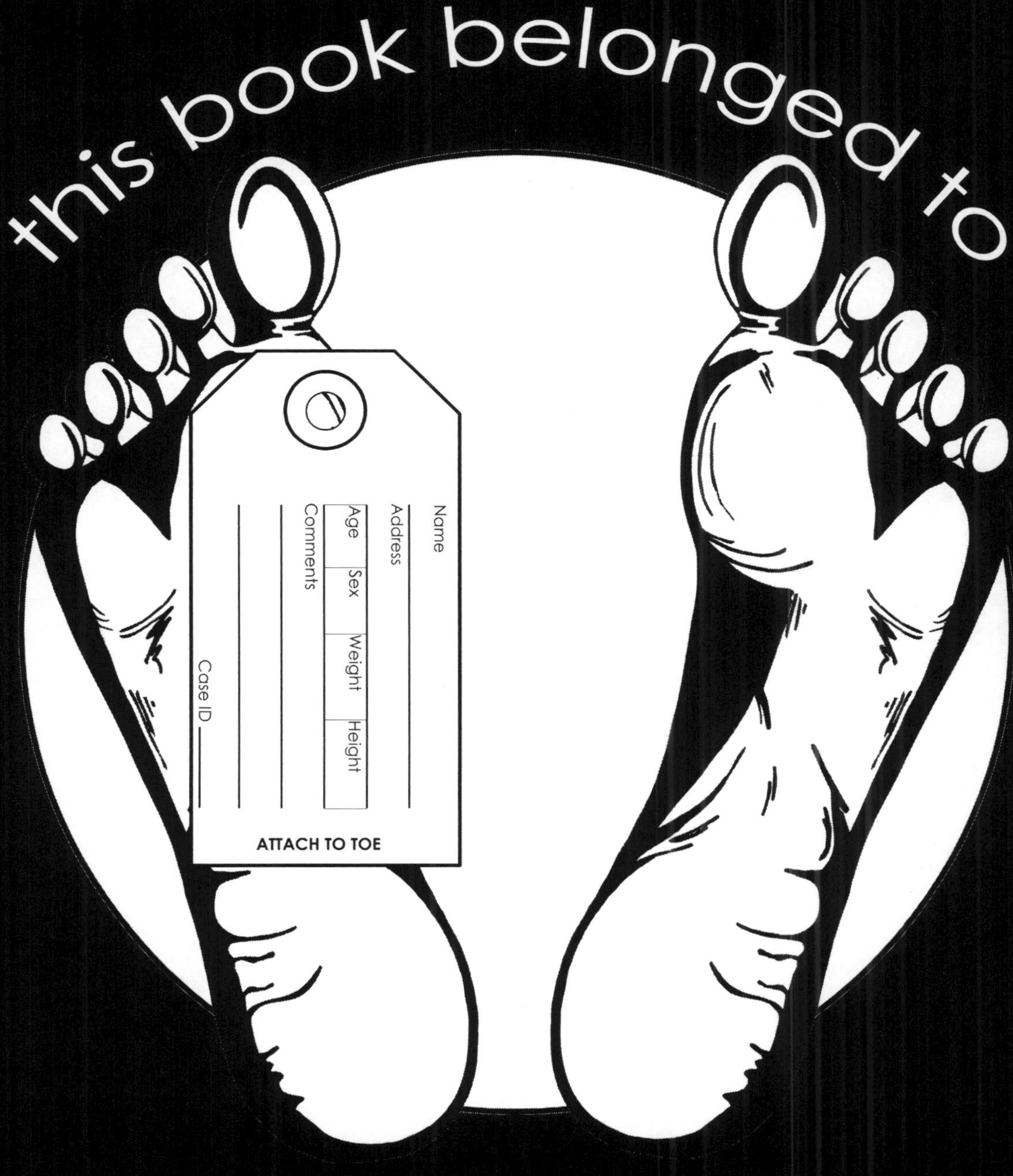
this book belonged to
Name
Address
Age
Sex
Weight
Height
Comments
Case ID
ATTACH TO TOE

The Grim Reaper's Simple Guide
to staying alive & avoiding your own untimely demise

Hello, there. Death here. I have a crappy job. No one's ever happy to see me, I work alone, there's no health plan and I ride a horse, for cryin' out loud. Let me tell you, I've seen it all and it's honestly not that hard to keep from making my acquaintance prematurely.

Just don't be fucking stupid. Simple. Lock your doors. Richard Chase told detectives that he took locked doors as a sign that he wasn't welcome, but unlocked doors were an invitation to come inside.

Travel in packs. Don't go first or last. Or, better yet, don't go at all. Keep a large group of expendable friends. Everyone's replaceable.

What's that? You're so interesting and have all these awesome hipster hobbies? Congratulations. Don't be an insufferable prick about it. If you absolutely insist on hunting (animals, mushrooms, ginseng, etc.), hiking, or jogging, I hope you're prepared to find a body, because you probably will. (You know, along those same lines, don't be a garbage collector. Alleys, day or night, are just as dangerous and unpleasant as the so-called "great" outdoors).

Finally (and need I say more than this?) the murderer is often the person who finds the body. Joggers and garbage men often find bodies. You do the math.

Are you well-versed in martial arts and self-defense? No? No problem. Invest in guns and pepper spray. Shoot first. Shoot a lot. If you hear a sound you can't identify, just lay down heavy, wild fire in every direction. Ammo is cheap. You can't ask questions if you're goddamn dead. (This, by the way, is terrible advice. Don't do this.)

Look down. What are you wearing right now? Do you want to die and/or be buried in this outfit? No? Great! Don't hitchhike. And, shiitake fucking mushrooms, don't pick one up either.

Cheese & rice, exercise a modicum of common sense.

Young? In love? Goody. Just as a courtesy, no PDA, please, and as a matter of self-interest, STAY OFF lover's lane! Bad things (not just *that*!) happen on lover's lane. Ever heard of the Texarcana "moonlight murders?" Well, in short, a Phantom Killer attacked 8 people within a span of 10 weeks. Just watch The Town That Dreaded Sundown. It's better than birth control.

I'll also say this: watch out for charming, smart people with disarmingly good looks. They're almost always, if nothing more sinister, assholes. Uh, Ted Bundy, anyone?

The simple fact of the matter is that you could cloister yourself in isolation and live a life of pious solitude, but I still can't guarantee your safety. Not even if you go on the offensive and off everyone in your address book preemptively.

A popular podcast* is touting the motto, "fuck politeness." Meaning, don't compromise your personal safety as a matter of courtesy to strangers. Solid advice. Just don't be a dick. Nobody likes a dick.

Although it's not really necessary to your survival, I strongly suggest taking a moment to compose a badass catchphrase which you can deliver once you've bested a would-be assassin. Remember Seattle jogger (what did I say about jogging?) Kelly Herron who coined the phrase, "Not today, motherfucker," after fighting off an attempted assault. (Damn fine work, Kelly). Write yours here:

_____

_____

_____

See you later....
Yours in death.
GR

*My Favorite Murder.

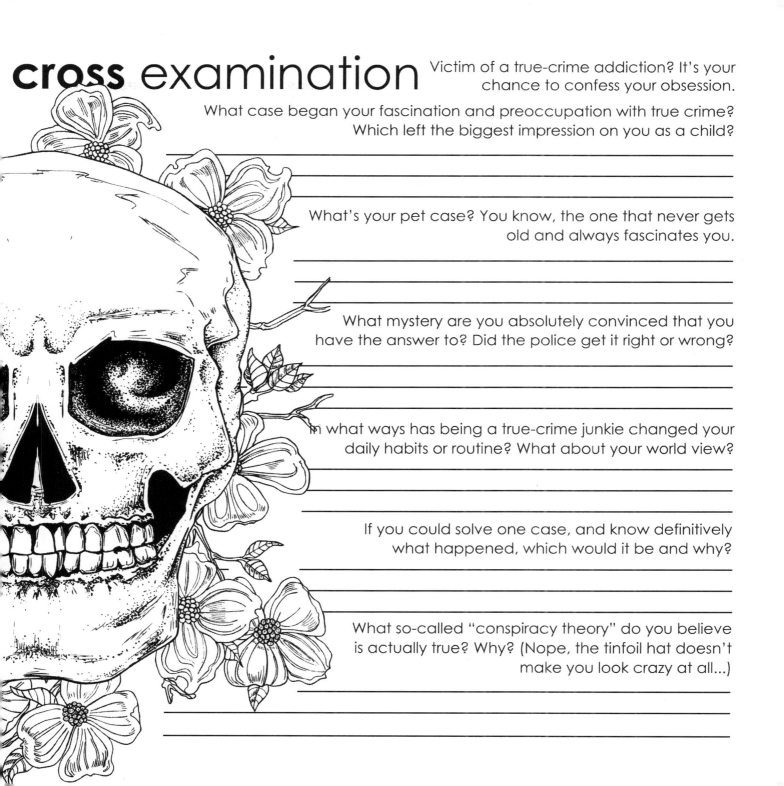

cross examination

Victim of a true-crime addiction? It's your chance to confess your obsession.

What case began your fascination and preoccupation with true crime? Which left the biggest impression on you as a child?

_____

_____

_____

What's your pet case? You know, the one that never gets old and always fascinates you.

_____

_____

What mystery are you absolutely convinced that you have the answer to? Did the police get it right or wrong?

_____

_____

_____

In what ways has being a true-crime junkie changed your daily habits or routine? What about your world view?

_____

_____

If you could solve one case, and know definitively what happened, which would it be and why?

_____

_____

What so-called "conspiracy theory" do you believe is actually true? Why? (Nope, the tinfoil hat doesn't make you look crazy at all...)

_____

_____

_____

If you vanished today, what wrong leads would police follow? Have you done anything recently that might be perceived as being out of character? Any people who might, incorrectly, be considered suspects in your disappearance because of temporary circumstances/unusual interactions?

_____

_____

_____

Which currently unsolved case(s) do you think will be solved in the next few years? What case are you surprised hasn't been solved yet?

_____

_____

_____

What case, even if it's solved, has left you completely baffled? Why does it keep you scratching your head?

_____

_____

_____

in the **dark**

This is a simple Caesar Cipher. The text is shifted by 21.

v	w	x	y	z	a	b	c	d	e	f	g	h	i	j	k	l	m	n	o	p	q	r	s	t	u
a	**b**	**c**	**d**	**e**	**f**	**g**	**h**	**i**	**j**	**k**	**l**	**m**	**n**	**o**	**p**	**q**	**r**	**s**	**t**	**u**	**v**	**w**	**x**	**y**	**z**

do'n vgrvtn ocz

nkjpnz!!

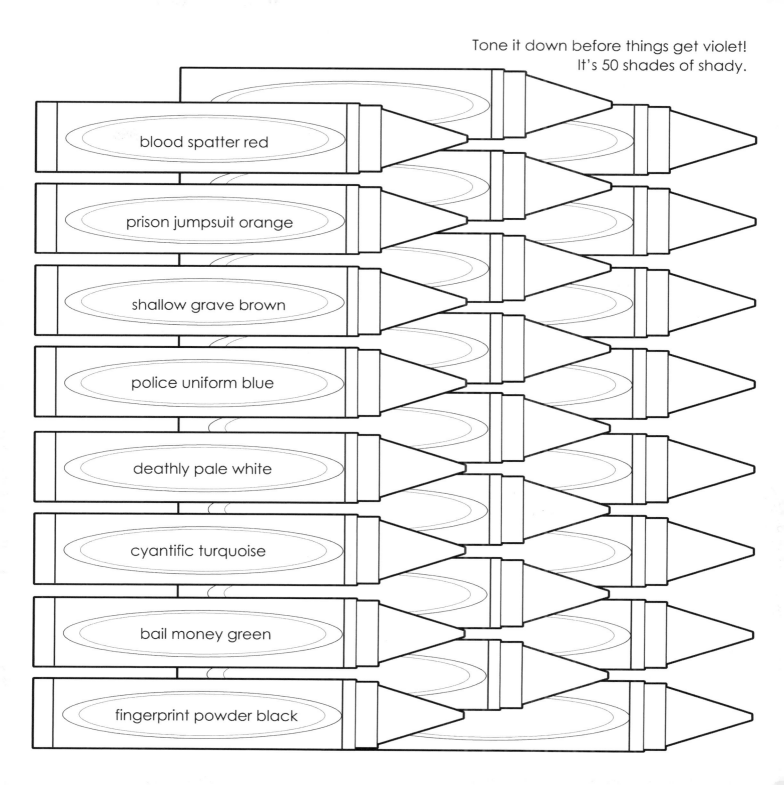

Tone it down before things get violet!
It's 50 shades of shady.

blood spatter red

prison jumpsuit orange

shallow grave brown

police uniform blue

deathly pale white

cyantific turquoise

bail money green

fingerprint powder black

It's a whole box of colorful crayons tailor-made for the murderino crowd. This was drawn at the suggestion of J. H. Adkins and her "to die for" boyfriend. You can download and print more copies for free (please do not use for profit or remove the watermark) at whatkatydrew.blogspot.com.

premeditated

Lots of cases are cracked because of small mistakes. List some classic examples of silly blunders & what simple fix you'd use to avoid the same pitfalls.

Use the back as needed to devise the perfect plan...

Jumping at shadows.
You hear a sound
as you're falling asleep.
Draw all of the things you
imagine it could be...

agora**phobe**

Karen knows that there are 25-50 active serial killers in the US right now.* *This very moment.* Karen also knows that 1 in 3 murders are unsolved.... Draw a picture of what Karen imagines is waiting just outside her front door.

*according to the former FBI Chief of Serial Crimes Unit, John Douglas,

caption this

stacked

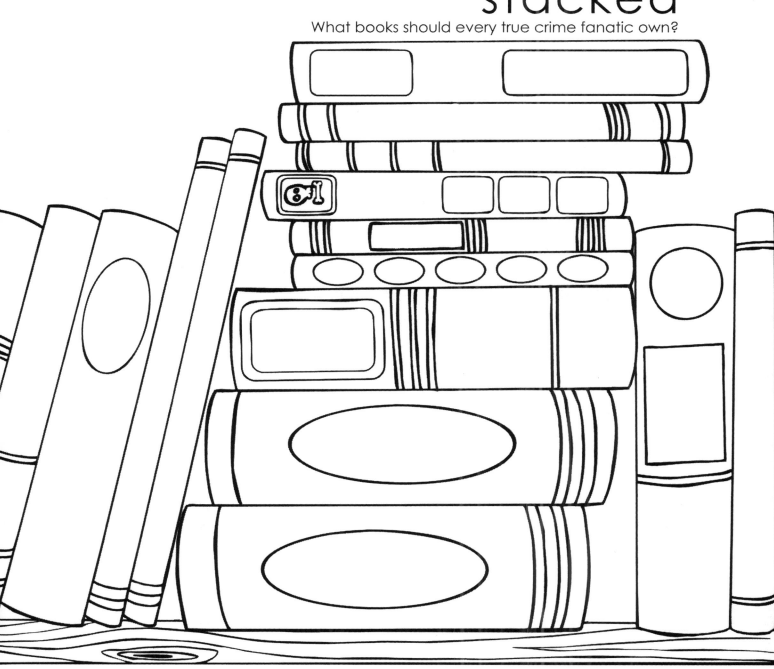

Last gasp. With her last breath, Holly utters her final words.

the road **death traveled**

A suspicious stranger pulls up alongside Jan.
Jan is smart. Jan knows not to accept rides from fuckwits.
Help her shut this shit down and get home safely to her cats.

emergency
preparedness
Take stock of the room you're in right now. Draw or list any make-shift weapons that you could use in a pinch.

bad trip

Your life flashes before your eyes;
everything comes into sharp focus.
List your greatest regrets below.

Use the back as needed.

netflix **and kill**

What true crime series are you binge-watching tonight? **Bonus:** What excuse did you give your friends to avoid hanging out and stay home alone?

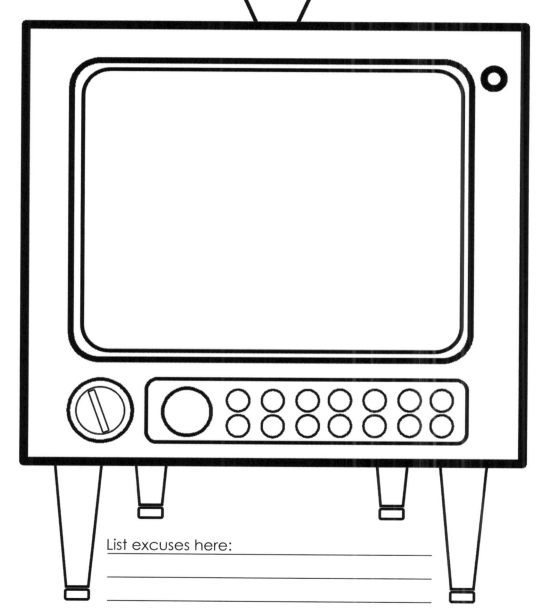

List excuses here: _____
_____
_____

Start a list of all the suspicious shit you see.
Be sure to note dates and times.

scared to **death**

What has this community more than a little on edge?

dear **diary**

Should I go missing or die under mysterious circumstances,
the following people should be investigated thoroughly.

_____

_____

_____

_____

stark graving mad.

This is Helene. Helene can't make connections with people because she knows that
serial killers look like everyone else and are able to hide in plain sight.
You need to relax the fuck down, Helene. Don't be like Helene.

last meal

It's your final fare.
What's on your plate?

framed!

Who's taking the rap for your shady crap?
Frame someone you don't like below.

now i lay me
down to sleep

List and/or illustrate all the things
keeping you awake at night.

armchair **detective**

Embellish the armchair
you're solving crimes from.
What's on the coffee table?
Be honest. Is it popcorn?

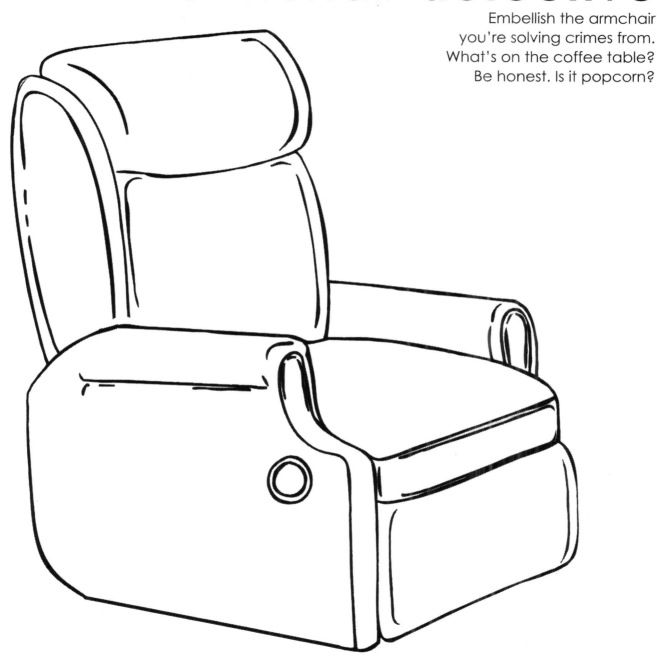

dead **bolt**

Secure this front door. Lock it down like Fort Knox, baby! Add a bolt, padlock, and perhaps even a peephole. Will you be adding a mail slot? What are your thoughts or observations on sliding glass doors? Might as well just sign your death certificate right now, amiright?

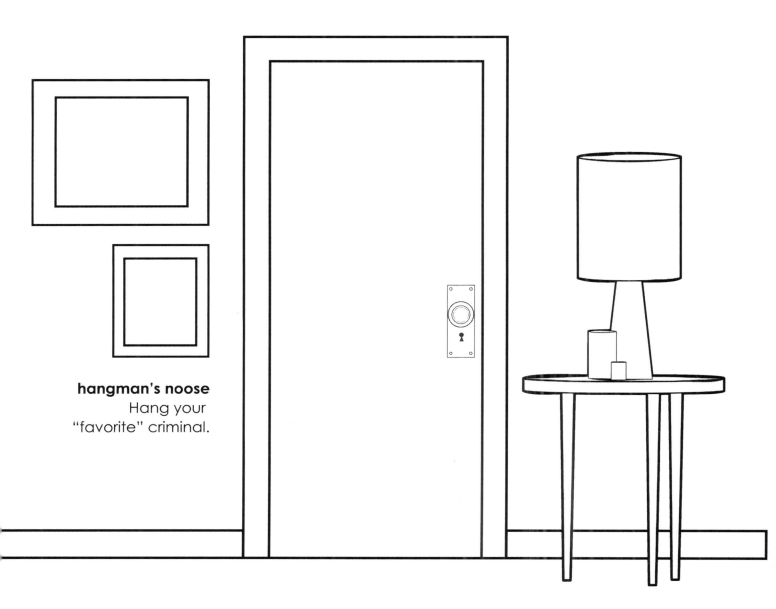

hangman's noose
Hang your
"favorite" criminal.

overanalyze things

Val hasn't heard from her sister in, like, an hour. Imagine all the terrible things that could have happened to her.

deathbed **confession**

Don't take shit with you to the grave.
You're being a selfish dick!* What shocking
revelation does Kelly make on her deathbed?
*So say the hosts of the My Favorite Murder Podcast.

judge, jury and **executioner**

Jo is an armchair detective. Jo's super good at making assumptions and figuring stuff out. Probably because she's seen *all* the TV and read *all* the books. She's always in chat rooms online. In what case is Jo certain that someone got away with murder? In what case has the family of a victim not appeared to be suitably distraught, at least to Jo's satisfaction? What does her post history look like? Help Jo draw some conclusions and spread wild speculation below.

a view to **kill**

Meredith drops eaves (not cool, Meredith, not cool). What did she see/overhear that she shouldn't have?

shoot the breeze

Phyllis is at a party. She shoots herself in the foot. (Or puts her foot in her mouth. Either way, what an amateur). What random piece of serial killer trivia does Phyllis share that guarantees she won't be invited back?

conspiracy theory

In which case are you convinced a dark plot lurks - hidden in plain sight so brilliantly that only crackpots & nuts believe it? In fact, their staunch defense of it only makes it seem all the more unbelievable. Is it a cover-up? Incompetence? Corruption? Lay out your case below.

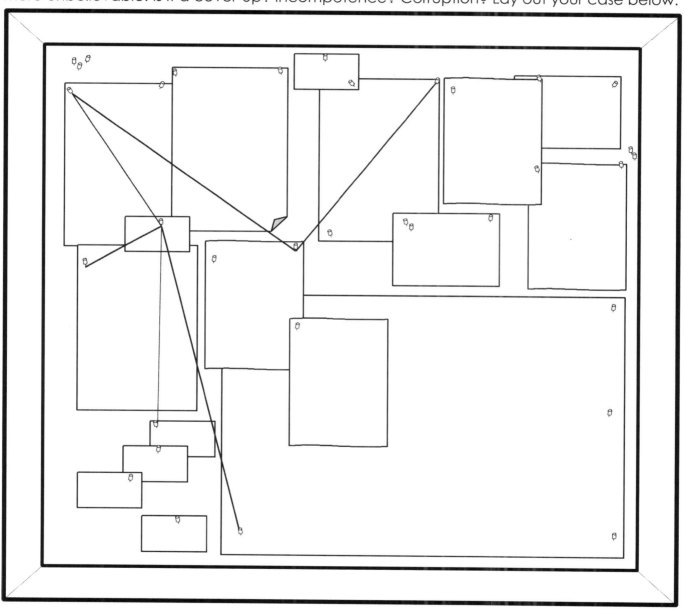

cootie catcher

Use this paper fortune teller to determine and avoid your fate. Outlive everyone you know simply by asking the right questions. By the way, this miraculous little piece of omnipotent origami is so-called because (and this is according to the infallible and all-knowing Wikipedia), it "may be used as a pincer to play-act catching insects such as lice, hence the "cootie catcher" name."

You can fold yours according to the directions below or check out a video tutorial at whatkatydrew.blogspot.com.

1. Begin by carefully removing your cootie-catcher from the book. Cut off any excess white portions surrounding the illustrations. Be sure to trim it into a square. A rectangle will not fold correctly. Color and decorate as desired.

2. Fold your paper diagonally in half across each corner (fold along the dotted lines shown here at left.)

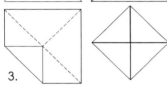

3. Fold each corner up to the middle point.

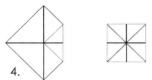

4. Flip the paper upside-down so that all the folded seams are facing down. Using the creases as guidelines, again fold each corner up to the middle point. You're almost there! Now, simply fold and unfold the paper horizontally and vertically.

5. Insert your fingers into the 4 pockets created by the corners of folded paper meeting in the middle point on the backside. Gently pull or lift the corners up and away from the middle point. The paper should now form a free-standing salt cellar shape. Congratulations! You're ready to play!

Game Play: With all 4 fingers pinched together, choose, or have a friend choose, one of the 4 options. In this case, "witch, monster, alien, or undead." Spell the word they've picked by moving the points of the catcher together and apart, sort of like a mouth. The catcher will be open to a another set of choices. "dice, runes, crystal ball, or eight ball," or "astrology, tea leaves, tarot, or palmistry." Again, make a choice and spell the word. You'll be presented with a final set of choices. Make your selection from the options available. Remove your fingers and lift the flap to reveal the fortune hidden beneath your final selection. Good luck.

To see a video of game play, visit www.whatkatydrew.blogspot.com.

dressed **to kill**

Angela is entering the witness protection program. Give her a killer disguise & bitchin' wardrobe.

Carefully cut and mount on construction paper or cardstock or something. I don't know. I'm not martha fucking stewart.

in your face!

"demure"der

knuckle sandwich

if looks could kill...

have a cat? of course she does.

skeleton in the closet

murder by design

This merry murderess is in complete control.

1	red	5	dark blue	9	black
2	peach/flesh	6	light green	10	brown
3	pink	7	dark green		
4	light blue	8	grey		

blank is white

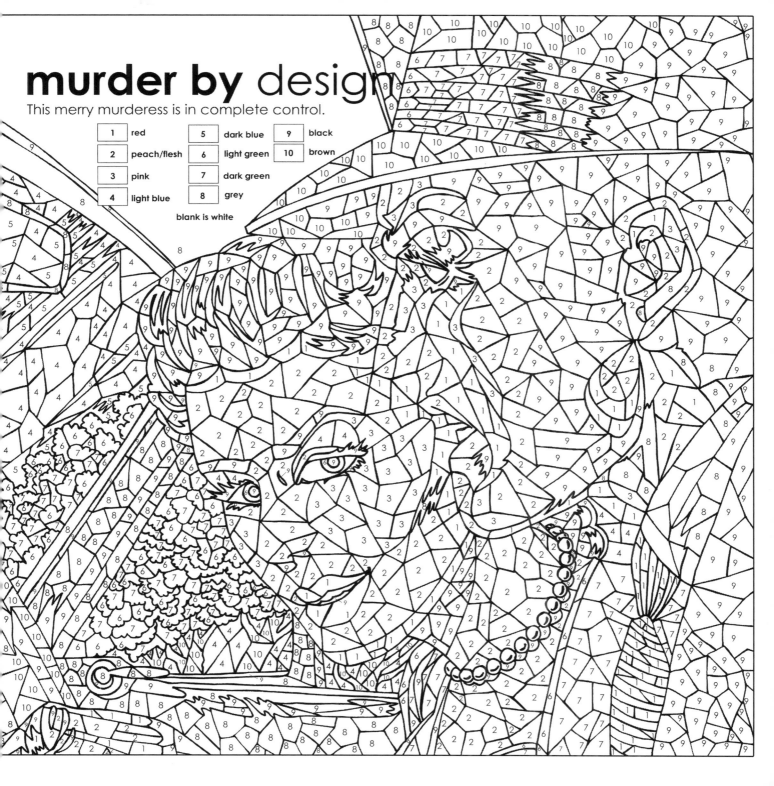

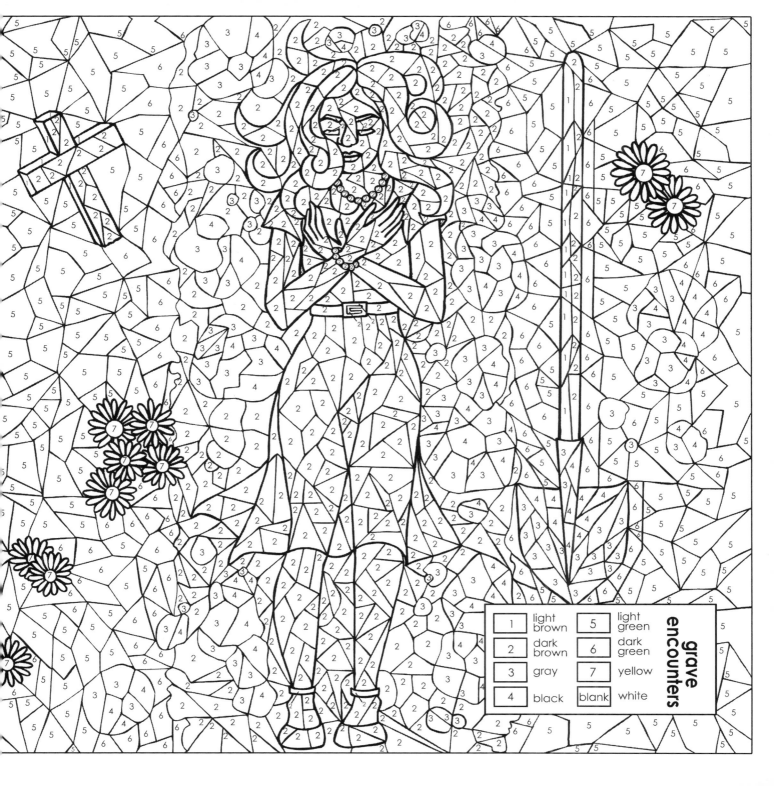

grave encounters

1	light brown	
2	dark brown	
3	gray	
4	black	
5	light green	
6	dark green	
7	yellow	
blank	white	

apprehend
the **asshole**

According to npr.org, the clearance rate for homicide is only 64.1%. Connect the dots and close this case.

"iconic" killer

Based on only the image below, identify the asshole. Answers are upside-down below.

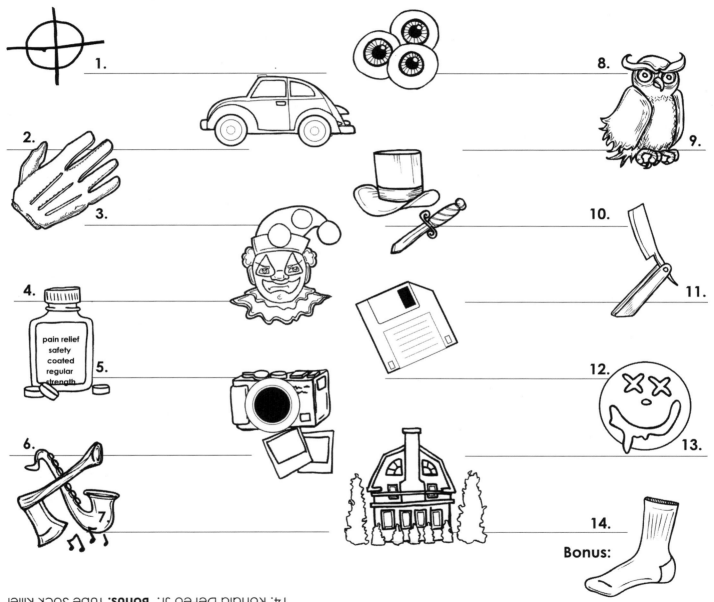

1. _____
2. _____
3. _____
4. _____
5. _____
6. _____
7. _____
8. _____
9. _____
10. _____
11. _____
12. _____
13. _____
14. _____

Bonus:

pain relief
safety
coated
regular
strength

smoking **gun**

According to the FBI, below shown are the most commonly used murder weapons. Rank them in the correct order of use from 1-10.

poison

fire

knife

shotgun

rifle

personal weapon
(hand, fist, feet, etc)

explosives

handgun

narcotics

blunt object

down and out

Connect the murderer and their last meal.

1. Albert Fish
2. Aileen Wuornos
3. John Wayne Gacy
4. HH Holmes
5. Timothy McVeigh
6. Allen Lee Davis
7. Christopher Brooks
8. Victor Feguer
9. Saddam Hussein
10. Ted Bundy

A. You scream, I scream...
2 pints of mint chocolate chip ice cream.

C. Sunnyside up.
Steak, eggs, toast, hash browns.*

* It wasn't eaten.

F. Hardboiled.
Boiled eggs, dry toast, and coffee.

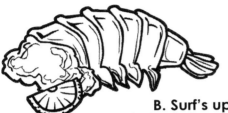

B. Surf's up.
Lobster tail, potatoes, shrimp, clams, and garlic bread.

D. T-bone.
Steak.

E. There's no wrong way to eat a Reeses?
Reeses peanut butter cups, and Dr. Pepper.

G. Finger lickin' good.
(This one's too easy...)
A bucket of KFC, fried shrimp, french fries, and 1/2 lb of strawberries.

I. Foul mood.
Chicken, rice, and hot water with honey.

J. It's the pits.
A single olive with a pit.

But first, coffee

H. I'd kill for a cuppa.
A cup of black coffee.

prove it!

Use the evidence below to prove the case beyond a reasonable doubt.
Connect the types of evidence and the examples of them.
Are they (A) Admissible or (I) Inadmissible

1. Exculpatory Evidence

2. Hearsay

3. Expert Testimony

4. Prima Facie Evidence

5. Character Evidence

6. Digital Evidence

7. Demonstrative Evidence

8. Testimony

9. Inculpatory Evidence

10. Circumstantial Evidence

11. Physical Evidence

A. Demonstrates or proves a person's involvement in a crime by generally indicating or proving guilt

B. Relies on an inference to connect it to a conclusion of fact —like a fingerprint at the scene of a crime

C. Statements from witnesses not present in court

D. Photographs, videos, sound recordings, x-rays, maps, drawings, graphs, animations, charts, sculptures, and models

E. Dried blood, fingerprints, weapons, DNA samples, fingerprints, plaster casts of footprints or tires, handprints, tool marks

F. Spoken or written evidence given by a witness under oath in court, at a deposition, or in an affidavit

G. Information favoring the defendant, either partially or completely proving their innocence

H. Emails, hard drives, digital photographs, word processing documents, spreadsheets, browser histories, instant messages, ATM transactions, GPS tracking, and cell phone logs

I. Demonstrates that a person has a certain personality trait and that they acted in a way consistent with that trait

J. Literally meaning "on first appearance," it means that upon an initial exam, enough evidence seems to exist to support a case

K. Testimony made by a qualified person about a scientific, technical, or professional issue

1. G 2. C 3. K 4. J 5. I 6. H 7. D 8. F 9. A 10. B 11. E

dead end

Connect the serial killer and their fate. Answers at the bottom of the page.

1. Jeffrey Dahmer

2. Ted Bundy

3. John Wayne Gacy

4. Ed Gein

5. HH Holmes

6. Edmund Kemper

7. Israel Keyes

8. Long Island Serial Killer (LISK)

9. Original Night Stalker /East Area Rapist

10. Phantom Killer

11. Dennis Rader

12. Richard Ramirez

13. Gary Ridgway

14. Aileen Wuornos

15. The Zodiac Killer

A. Bludgeoned to death in prison by fellow inmates on November 28, 1994.

B. A fan of cryptograms, this killer taunted police but vanished in 1974 and the California case file remains open to this day.

C. Believed to have murdered 10 to 17 people associated with prostitution over a period of nearly 20 years. This killer remains unidentified.

D. Committed suicide in prison before sharing his total victim count and the location of their bodies.

E. Credited with attacking eight people within ten weeks, five of whom were killed, this killer has never been caught.

F. Currently serving 48 life sentences in a Washington prison without the possibility of parole.

G. Currently serving ten consecutive life sentences in a Kansas jail.

H. Despite committing over 50 attacks and 10 murders, he remains at large to this day.

I. Died at age 53 awaiting execution at San Quentin Prison.

J. Died in a mental facility in 1984 & buried in an unmarked grave.

K. Executed by electric chair at Florida State Prison Jan. 24, 1989.

L. Executed by lethal injection on October 9, 2002.

M. Hanged at the Philadelphia County Prison on May 7, 1896. Buried in 10 feet of cement to thwart grave robbers.

N. Requested the death penalty, but received 8 life sentences being served in the general population of a California jail.

O. Spent 14 years on death row before being executed by lethal injection on May 10, 1994.

check, **please!**

Why is Pam putting on her coat? Pam's dinner companion has made the following statements. Diagnose them as being the behavior of a "P" psychopath, "S" sociopath, "B" both, or "N" "normal." Circle the point at which she demanded the check?

1. "That's okay, laws just don't apply to me."

2. "Calm down? You calm down! Oh, sorry, it's just that I'm a little anxious. My last girlfriend told me that I'm prone to emotional outbursts. Obviously that's complete bullshit!"

3. "Yes, in fact, I *have* been told that I have a disarming personality. I've been accused of being ridiculously & obscenely charming."

4. "Stick with me, babe. I always get my way. I'm a master manipulator. Watch this. 'Hey! Waitress! Could I get a discount on this?'"

5. "Yeah, sure I did it, but I don't feel bad about it AT ALL. They had it coming'."

6. "I'm a real jack-of-all trades. Got lots of skills. I've worked 9 jobs in 2 years. My bosses never appreciate me."

7. "Well, when plan A didn't work out, I just went to plan B. Actually, I had to use plan K, but it was fine. I'd made all the necessary arrangements. "

8. "I'm a fly-by-the-seat of my pants kinda guy. I'm super spontaneous. I don't make plans."

9. "No worries, baby. It's fine; I'm not mad. I never get mad."

1. B/both
2. S/sociopath
3. P/psychopath
4. P/psychopath
5. B/both
6. S/sociopath
7. P/psychopath
8. S/sociopath
9. P/psychopath

pick your **poison**

Diagnose the common & dangerous poison.

a. polonium	c. household cleaners	e. cyanide	g. anti-freeze	i. carbon monoxide
b. hemlock	d. acetaminophen	f. methanol	h. belladonna	k. botulinum toxin

1. Meaning "beautiful woman" in Italian, it was used in the middle ages as a sort of cosmetic product. Even just a single leaf is lethal. Eating 10 of the berries would also be fatal.

2. Second-leading cause (behind cosmetics & personal care products) of poison exposure in children, says CNN.

3. The leading cause of poisoning death, says the CDC. It's colorless, odorless. and causes sudden illness or death. It's is often detected only when it's too late.

4. Midol, Tylenol, Excedrin, Pamprin, Mucinex, & Robitussin result in 500 deaths per year because of this common ingredient. Do not exceed 3,000 mg per day.

5. This radioactive poison was used in a cup of tea to kill former Russian spy Alexander Litvinenko. A single gram vaporized into the air could kill over 1 million people.

6. A highly toxic type of alcohol, which, if consumed can cause permanent blindness and death.

7. Sweet tasting, this poison can be deadly in small doses. Difficult to diagnose because symptoms are varied. Requires prompt medical treatment.

8. Described in fiction as having a "bitter almond" smell, but it doesn't always have an odor, & not everyone can detect it anyway, says the CDC.

9. Highly toxic flowering plant. A dose of only about 8 leaves is fatal – you're awake, but your body is paralysed & you slowly stop breathing.

10. Injected to cosmetically mask signs of aging. If ingested, it causes paralysis of the respiratory system and death

1.h. 2.c. 3.i. 4.d. 5.a. 6.f. 7.g. 8.e 9.b. 10.k

on the **case**

Locate & decipher the clues. Don’t the let trail go cold!

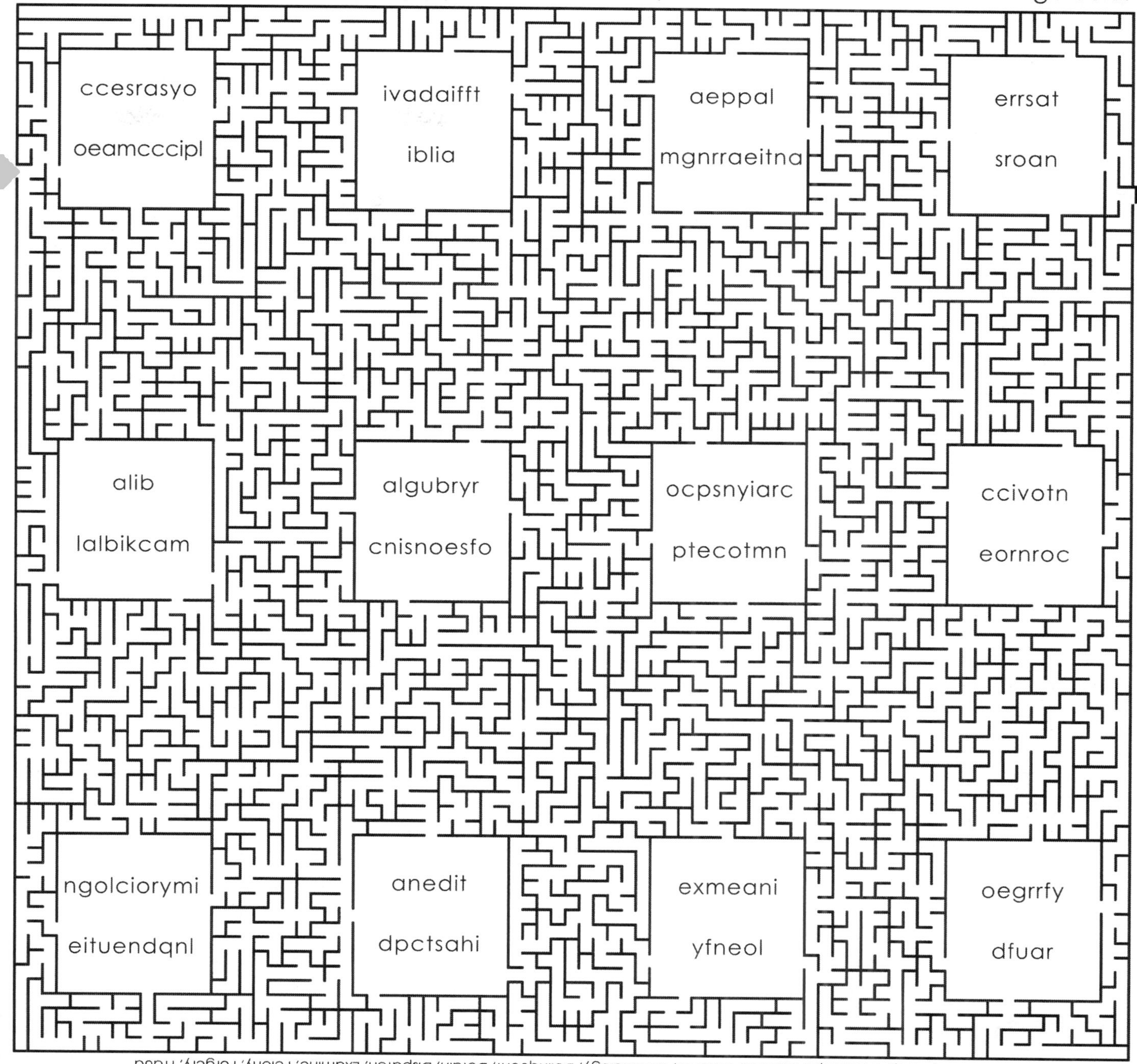

ccesrasyo
oeamcccipl
ivadaifft
iblia
aeppal
mgnrraeitna
errsat
sroan
alib
lalbikcam
algubryr
cnisnoesfo
ocpsnyiarc
ptecotmn
ccivotn
eornroc
ngolciorymi
eituendqnl
anedit
dpctsahi
exmeani
yfneol
oegrrfy
dfuar

Accessory, Accomplice, Affidavit, Alibi, Appeal, Arraignment, Arrest, Arson, Bail, Blackmail, Burglary, Confession,
Conspiracy, Contempt, Convict, Coroner, Criminology, Delinquent, Detain, Dispatch, Examine, Felony, Forgery, Fraud

jail break

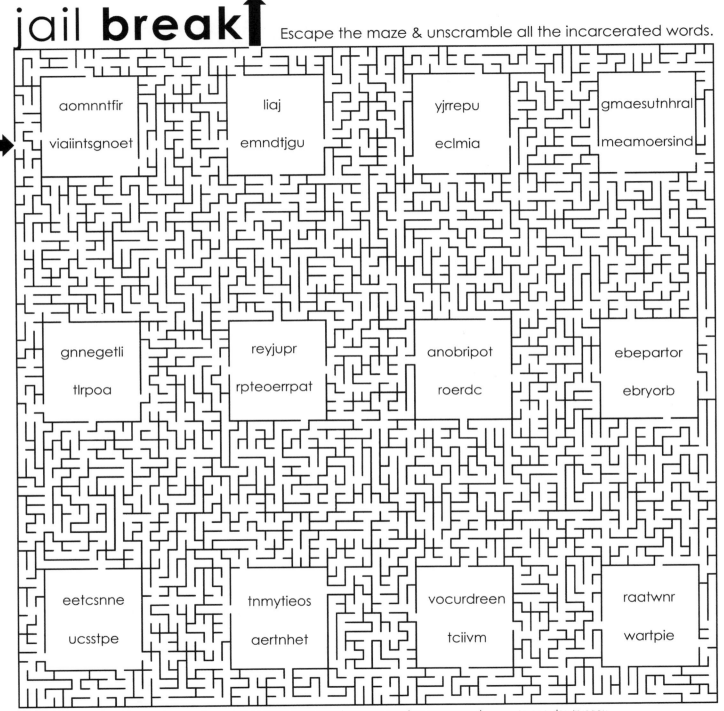

Escape the maze & unscramble all the incarcerated words.

aomnntfir
viaiintsgnoet

liaj
emndtjgu

yjrrepu
eclmia

gmaesutnhral
meamoersind

gnnegetli
tlrpoa

reyjupr
rpteoerrpat

anobripot
roerdc

ebepartor
ebryorb

eetcsnne
ucsstpe

tnmytieos
aertnhet

vocurdreen
tciivm

raatwnr
wartpie

Informant, Investigation, Jail, Judgment, Jury, Perjury, Malice, Manslaughter, Misdemeanor, Negligent, Patrol, Perjury, Perpetrator, Probation, Record, Reprobate, Robbery, Sentence, Suspect, Testimony, Threaten, Undercover Victim, Warrant, Wiretap

Word list:

arson
attorney
autopsy
ballpeenhammer
bazooka
bluntforcetrauma
bomb
brassknuckles
candlestick
clues
coldcase
crimescene
criminal
dagger
defenestration
derringer
detective
drowning
explosives
fingerprints
forensic
garrote
homicide
icePick
investigation
knife
leadpipe
machinegun
mallet
medicalexaminer
mugshot
murder
mystery
pepperspray
perpetrator
pistol
poison
police
privateeye
prosecutor
redherring
reporter
revolver
robbery
rope
stalker
strangle
suspect
sword
unsolved

dead **reckoning**

As if you don't have anything better to do. Unscramble the following euphemisms for falling off your perch, having a hand in your dinner pail, joining the invisible choir...You know, idioms for death and dying.

okcar _____	ddae sa a rondoail _____
steo up _____	og otu twhi a abgn _____
urtsnica _____	ried eht elap hoser _____
lybel pu _____	lafl ffo uory rchpe _____
gep tuo _____	tguhob eht amfr _____
eepd ixs _____	vegi up eth shtgo _____
pu nad ied _____	a etasx kelakacw _____
sedhac uot _____	pop oyur clsog _____
irtd pan _____	tkea yoru lats wbo _____
tenldlifa _____	itocugnn msrow _____
acll it iqtus _____	srcso hte ergat dviied _____
fbrtee of flei _____	tewn eth wya of all eflhs _____
aetk a trdi npa _____	oen ootf in hte ergav _____
iyaglpn a aphr _____	arwe a eipn vaoteroc _____
lacl off lal steb _____	sih bnmeru aws up _____
utp ot peles _____	selpe twih hte esfsih _____
feufsnd uto _____	ghtbou a eon ayw titkec _____
isx etfe ednru _____	kkedci eht oynexg bhiat _____
otu fo bsiesusn _____	simw whit ctcoeren hesso _____
pshu up iissaed _____	*bored to death?*

case file

How many words can you make using only the letters in the word "**detective**?" I'll go first. "vice."

_____ _____ _____
_____ _____ _____
_____ _____ _____
_____ _____ _____
_____ _____ _____
_____ _____ _____

dead reckoning

Scrambled	Answer
okcar	Croak
steo up	Toes up
urtsnica	Curtains
lybel pu	Belly Up
gep tuo	Peg Out
eepd ixs	Deep Six
pu nad ied	Up and Die
sedhac uot	Cashed Out
irtd pan	Dirt Nap
tenldlifa	Flatlined
acll it iqtus	Call It Quits
fbrtee of flei	Bereft of Life
take a trdi nap	Take a Dirt Nap
iyaglpn a aphr	Playing a Harp
lacl off lal steb	Call Off All Bets
utp ot peles	Put to Sleep
feufsnd uto	Snuffed Out
isx feet ednru	Six Feet Under
out of bsiesusn	Out of Business
pshu up iissaed	Push Up Daisies

Scrambled	Answer
ddae sa a rondoail	Dead as a Doornail
og otu twhi a abgn	Go out With a Bang
ried eht elap hoser	Ride the Pale Horse
lafl ffo uory rchpe	Fall off Your Perch
tguhob eht amfr	Bought the Farm
vegi up eth shtgo	Give up the Ghost
a etasx kelakacw	A Texas Cakewalk
pop oyur clsog	Pop Your Clogs
tkea yoru lats wbo	Take Your Last Bow
itocugnn msrow	Counting Worms
srcso hte ergat dviied	Cross the Great Divide
tewn eth wya of all eflhs	Went the Way of all Flesh
oen ootf in hte ergav	One Foot in the Grave
arwe a eipn vaoteroc	Wear a Pine Overcoat
sih bnmeru aws up	His Number was Up
selpe twih hte esfsih	Sleep with the Fishes
ghtbou a eon ayw titkec	Bought a One Way Ticket
kkedci eht oynexg bhiat	Kicked the Oxygen Habit
simw whit ctcoeren hesso	Swim with Concrete Shoes

nailed it!

take a **stab at it**

Transform the following words from one word to another in as few steps as possible. Change only one letter at a time. For example, go from File to Bind: File, Mile, Mine, Mind, Bind.

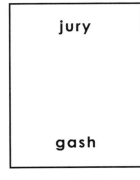

buried

dumped

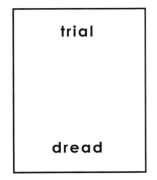

jury

gash

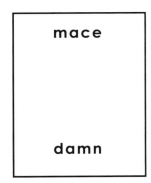

trial

dread

mace

damn

buried, burped, bumped, dumped. jury, bury, busy, bush, bash, gash. trial, triad, tread, dread. mace, face, fame, dame, damn.

v ypgg fidaz dn v yvibzmjpn fidaz

grave expectations

It's the most popular place in town. I mean, everyone's dying to get in. (Sorry about that. Just a bit of gallows humor - I couldn't resist.) Unscramble all these cemetery synonyms. You know, a permanent retirement home, mother nature's acres, the toes-up motel, pushing-up daisies patch...you get the idea.

ebno uyoba _____	oarylgeg geaagr _____
dbyraoen _____	gthso nowt _____
eoonbzne _____	verga-otl _____
raulib nudmo _____	lodawlhe rugond _____
yrbu capht _____	lahelowd shlil _____
arcdeva prak _____	amrbel lmal _____
cyti of slnaeg _____	rioecnpslo _____
noficf omooshrw _____	epin oxb claepa _____
codl tefe laglevi _____	pleca fo on errunt _____
ropsec pedot _____	etotrp's elifd _____
odcrassors _____	mroo tiuthow a eiwv _____
crow saontit _____	lsluk rrhocad _____
edda amodin _____	fsift ticy _____
theda's arorlp _____	het tuds inb _____
itoypdesro _____	teh axt ehtserl _____
drti utsavl _____	btom wnto _____
tuds cyfrota _____	npurti htacp _____
gwaire arfm _____	nuerogddnur letho _____
afmyli plto _____	evylla fo het adde _____
oisslf marf _____	rwom apcth _____

manhunt

How many words can you make using only the letters in the word "**homicide**?" I'll go first. "medic."

_____ _____ _____
_____ _____ _____
_____ _____ _____
_____ _____ _____
_____ _____ _____
_____ _____ _____

grave expectations

ebno uyoba	Bone Bayou	oarylgeg geaagr	Gargoyle Garage
dbyraoen	Boneyard	gthso nowt	Ghost Town
eoonbzne	Bonezone	verga-otl	Grave-lot
raulib nudmo	Burial Mound	lodawlhe rugond	Hallowed Ground
yrbu capht	Bury Patch	lahelowd shlil	Hallowed Hills
arcdeva prak	Cadaver park	amrbel lmal	Marble Mall
cyti of slnaeg	City of Angels	rioecnpslo	Necropolis
noficf omooshrw	Coffin Showroom	epin oxb claepa	Pine Box Palace
codl tefe laglevi	Cold Feet Village	pleca fo on errunt	Place of no Return
ropsec pedot	Corpse Depot	etotrp's elifd	Potter's Field
odcrassors	Crossroads	mroo tiuthow a eiwv	Room Without a View
crow saontit	Crow Station	lsluk rrhocad	Skull Orchard
edda amodin	Dead Domain	fsift ticy	Stiff City
theda's arorlp	Death's Parlor	het tuds inb	The Dust Bin
itoypdesro	Depository	teh axt ehtserl	The Tax Shelter
drti utsavl	Dirt Vaults	btom wnto	Tomb Town
tuds cyfrota	Dust Factory	npurti htacp	Turnip Patch
gwaire arfm	Earwig Farm	nuerogddnur letho	Underground Hotel
afmyli plto	Family Plot	evylla fo het adde	Valley of the Dead
oisslf marf	Fossil Farm	rwom apcth	Worm Patch

Connect the dots below & CSI the shit out of this super scientific spatter analysis.

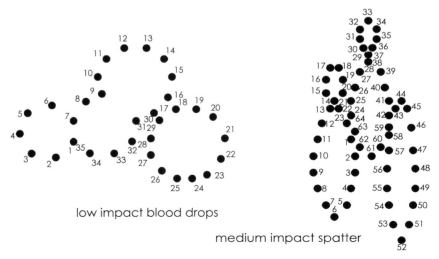

low impact blood drops

medium impact spatter

high impact spatter

CSI analysis

killer crossword

Across

1. Often wrongly touted as America's first female serial killer.
4. The Whitechapel Murderer who terrorized 19th century London.
7. Killer of the alleged assassin of President JFK.
11. Leader of the cult which committed mass suicide in Jonestown, Guyana.
12. Murdered John Lennon on December 8, 1980.
14. 6-foot-tall, 200 pound Norwegian-American serial killer. Allegedly faked her own death by fire.
15. Convicted rapist and serial killer appeared on (and won!) tv's The Dating Game as 'Bachelor #2.'
17. 'Took an axe and gave her mother 40 whacks.'

Down

2. Alleged Assassin of President JFK.
3. Spent 4 years in Italian prison before being acquitted of killing her British roommate.

Down (con't)

5. Notorious unidentified murderer with an affinity for letter writing and cryptograms.
6. Nicknamed 'the Juice.'
8. Appeared in 2015 HBO series "The Jinx" in which he allegedly admitted to murder.
9. Found not guilty of murdering her 2-year-old daughter in Florida.
10. Entertainer Pogo the Clown.
13. The Butcher of Plainfield.
16. Jazz loving 'demon' active from 1918-1919. _____ of New Orleans.

killer crossword

Across
1. aileen wuornos
4. jack the ripper
7. jack ruby
11. jim jones
12. mark david chapman
14. belle gunness
15. rodney alcala
17. lizzie borden*

Down
2. lee harvey oswald
3. amanda knox*
5. the zodiac killer
6. oj simpson*
8. robert durst
9. casey anthony*
10. john wayne gacy
13. ed gein
16. axeman

*acquitted

Transform the following words from one word to another in as few steps as possible.
Change only one letter at a time. For example, from File to Bind: File, Mile, Mine, Mind, Bind.

judge	stalk	cops	jail
sarge	scare	type	warn

judge, budge, badge, barge, sarge.   stalk, stark, snark, snare, scare.   cops, mops, mope, hope, hype, type.   jail, wail, wait, warn, warn.

on the
case

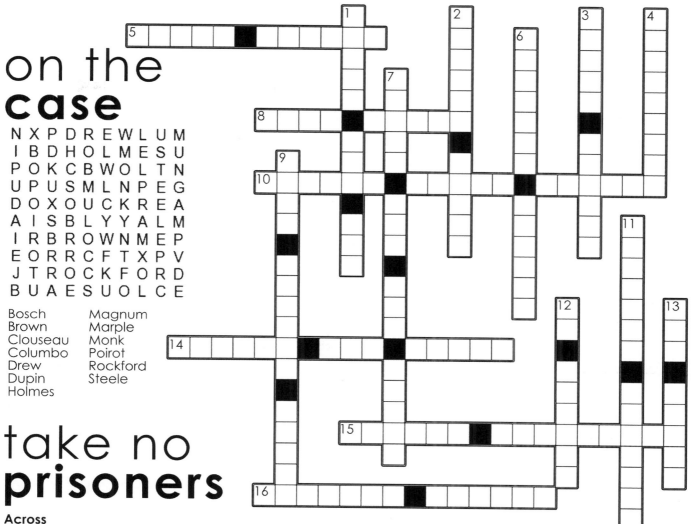

```
N X P D R E W L U M
I B D H O L M E S U
P O K C B W O L T N
U P U S M L N P E G
D O X O U C K R E A
A I S B L Y Y A L M
I R B R O W N M E P
E O R R C F T X P V
J T R O C K F O R D
B U A E S U O L C E
```

Bosch   Magnum
Brown   Marple
Clouseau   Monk
Columbo   Poirot
Drew   Rockford
Dupin   Steele
Holmes

take no
prisoners

Across
5. Nickname for aspiring actress Elizabeth Short.
8. LDS church convert who murdered her Arizona based LDS lover in the shower.
10. The East Area Rapist (EAR)/Original Night Stalker (ONS) was recently rebranded as 'The ____.'
14. 'The most notorious crime couple in American history died as they lived—in a hail of bullets.' - FBI
15. Shooter of Trayvon Martin, although he was later acquitted of second degree murder.
16. Pseudo-hippie cult leader who believed Helter Skelter to be an impending apocalyptic race war.

Down
2. Known as the BTK, 'Bind, Torture, Kill' Murderer.

Down (con't)
1. Folk hero & notorious outlaw of the American West born William H. Bonney.
3. Orange haired Dark Knight theater shooter.
4. Name for the murderer who mailed and planted bombs which killed three before his capture in 1996.
6. Cannibal from Milwaukee.
7. Convicted of killing Stephany Flores Ramirez in Peru. Suspected in the disappearance of Natalee Holloway.
9. Actor assassin of President Abraham Lincoln.
11. Satanist known as the Night Stalker.
12. Born Herman Webster Mudgett on May 16, 1861.
13. Volkswagen Beetle driving law student.

take no prisoners

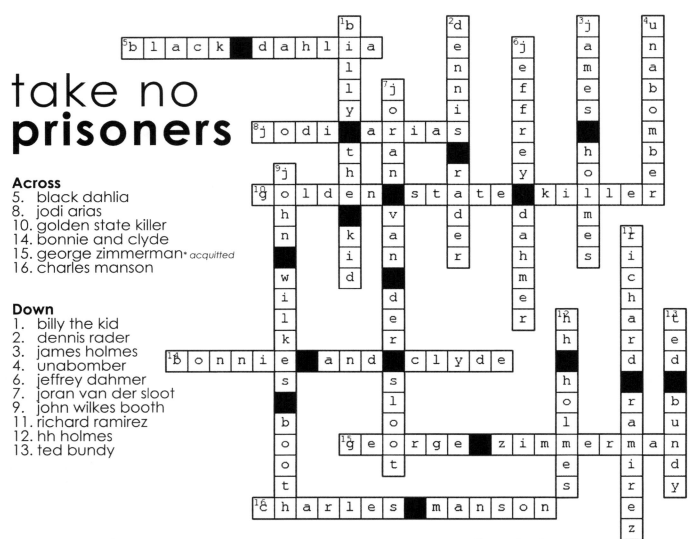

Across
5. black dahlia
8. jodi arias
10. golden state killer
14. bonnie and clyde
15. george zimmerman* *acquitted*
16. charles manson

Down
1. billy the kid
2. dennis rader
3. james holmes
4. unabomber
6. jeffrey dahmer
7. joran van der sloot
9. john wilkes booth
11. richard ramirez
12. hh holmes
13. ted bundy

on the case

bosch
brown
clouseau
columbo
drew
dupin
holmes

magnum
marple
monk
poirot
rockford
steele

tickle your funny bone

Two cryptographers walk into a bar...

ij jiz zgnz cvn vit dyzv rcvo oczt'mz
ovgfdib vwjpo!!

clue**less**

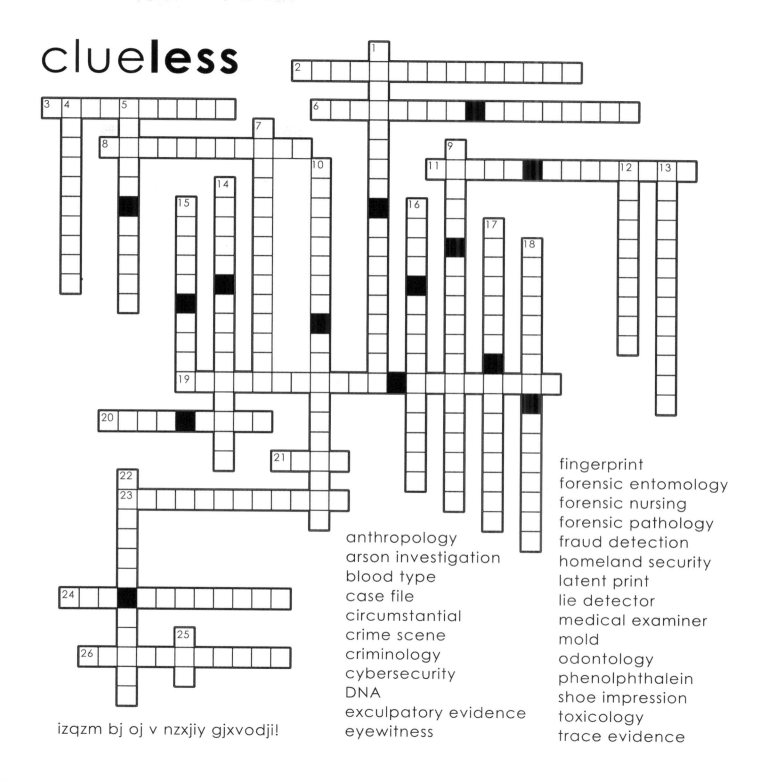

anthropology
arson investigation
blood type
case file
circumstantial
crime scene
criminology
cybersecurity
DNA
exculpatory evidence
eyewitness

fingerprint
forensic entomology
forensic nursing
forensic pathology
fraud detection
homeland security
latent print
lie detector
medical examiner
mold
odontology
phenolphthalein
shoe impression
toxicology
trace evidence

izqzm bj oj v nzxjiy gjxvodji!

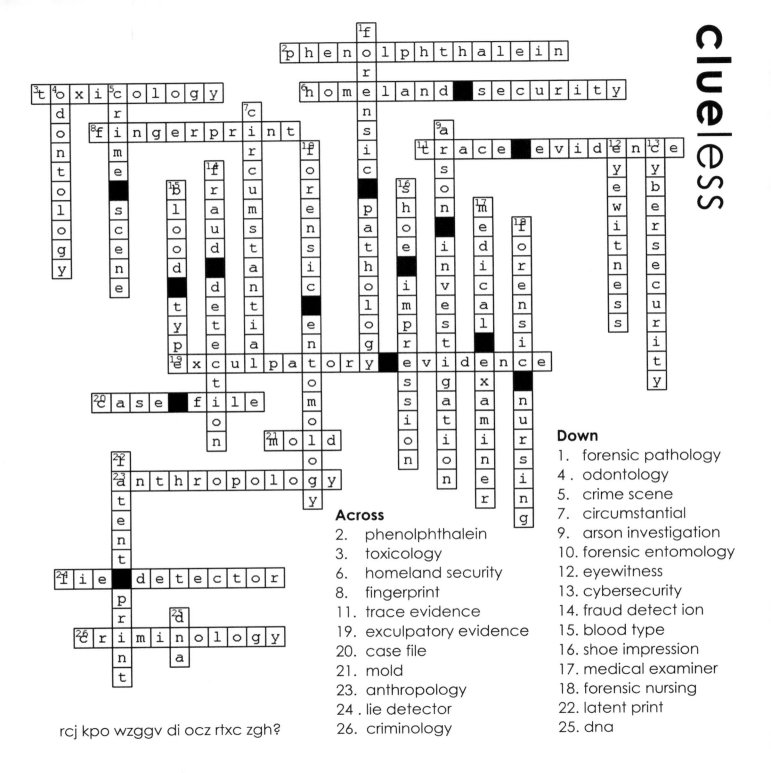

clueless

Across
2. phenolphthalein
3. toxicology
6. homeland security
8. fingerprint
11. trace evidence
19. exculpatory evidence
20. case file
21. mold
23. anthropology
24. lie detector
26. criminology

Down
1. forensic pathology
4. odontology
5. crime scene
7. circumstantial
9. arson investigation
10. forensic entomology
12. eyewitness
13. cybersecurity
14. fraud detect ion
15. blood type
16. shoe impression
17. medical examiner
18. forensic nursing
22. latent print
25. dna

rcj kpo wzggv di ocz rtxc zgh?

it's your **funeral**

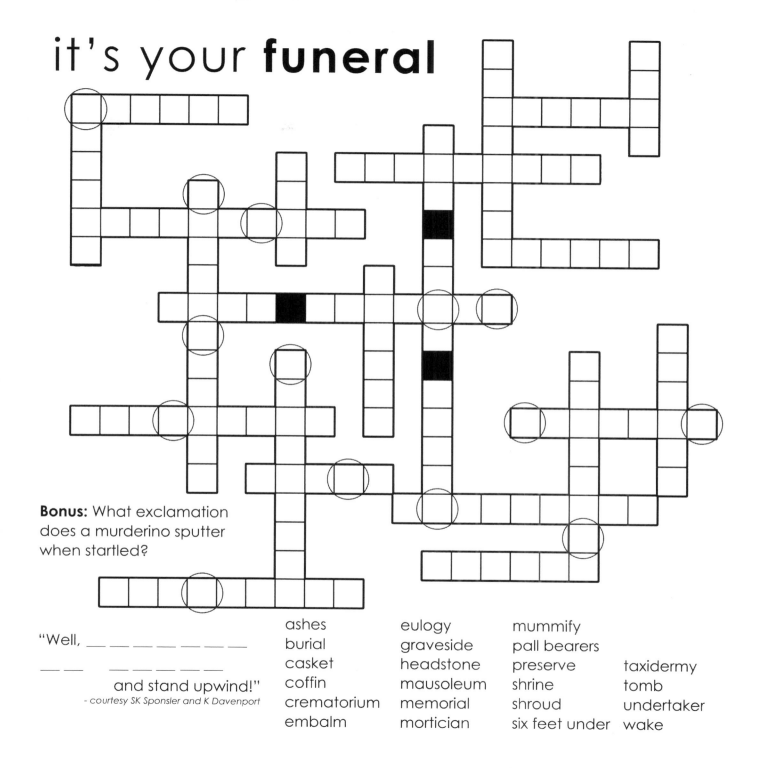

Bonus: What exclamation
does a murderino sputter
when startled?

"Well, _ _ _ _ _ _ _

_ _   _ _ _ _ _

and stand upwind!"
- *courtesy SK Sponsler and K Davenport*

ashes
burial
casket
coffin
crematorium
embalm

eulogy
graveside
headstone
mausoleum
memorial
mortician

mummify
pall bearers
preserve
shrine
shroud
six feet under

taxidermy
tomb
undertaker
wake

it's your **funeral**

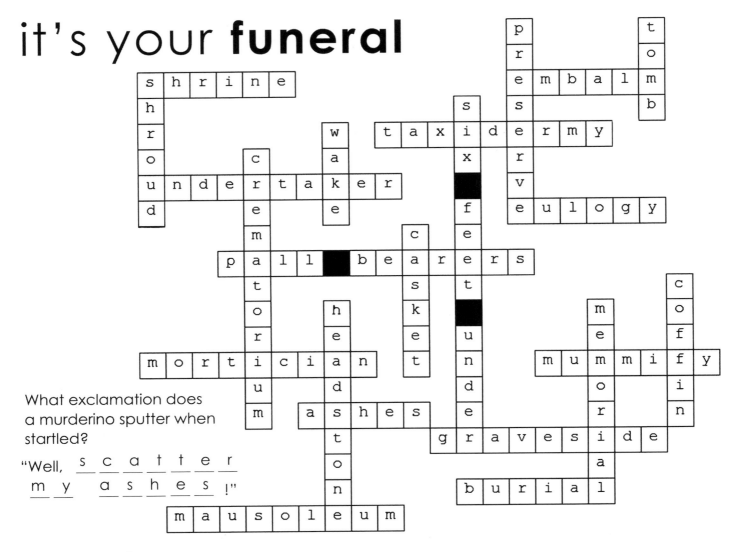

Crossword answers:
- shrine
- shroud (s-h-r-o-u-d vertical)
- undertaker
- taxidermy
- embalm
- tomb
- eulogy
- pallbearers
- mortician
- ashes
- headstone
- casket
- mummify
- coffin
- graveside
- burial
- mausoleum
- crematorium
- memorial
- cremate
- sarcophagus
- wake

What exclamation does a murderino sputter when startled?

"Well, s c a t t e r m y a s h e s !"

flatline

1. Near or at what core temperature will the heart stop and the body die of hypothermia?
2. How many days can the average person survive without water?
3. Near or at what core body temperature does severe hyperthermia occur?
4. How many weeks can the average person survive without food?
5. How many Gs of force can the average person withstand before losing consciousness?

survival advice. izqzm nkgdo pk

(upside down) 1 70 F 2. 3-4 days 3. 104 F 4. 3 weeks 5. five Gs

knock 'em dead

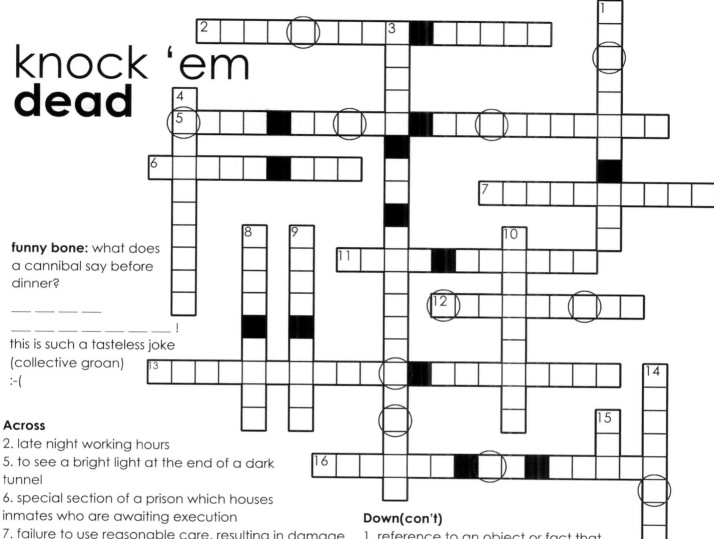

funny bone: what does a cannibal say before dinner?

__ __ __ __ __

__ __ __ __ __ __ __ __ __ !

this is such a tasteless joke (collective groan) :-(

Across
2. late night working hours
5. to see a bright light at the end of a dark tunnel
6. special section of a prison which houses inmates who are awaiting execution
7. failure to use reasonable care, resulting in damage or injury to another
11. personification of death in the form of a scythe wielding, cloak-wearing skeleton
12. to kill one's father
13. the killing of a person in circumstances without criminal guilt
16. frightened to the point of giving up one's ghost

Down
4. before death
10. to kill one's mother

Down(con't)
1. reference to an object or fact that serves as conclusive evidence of a crime
3. coroner's assessment indicating that death was an accidental result of dangerous risk taken voluntarily
8. process by which prospective jurors are questioned before being chosen to sit on a jury
9. animal(s) that has been struck and killed by motor vehicles on highways
14. mattress where upon a person takes their final breath
15. dead on arrival

knock 'em dead

Across
2. graveyard shift
5. near death experience
6. death row
7. negligence
11. grim reaper
12. patricide
13. justifiable homicide
16. scared to death

Down
1. smoking gun
3. death by misadventure
4. antemortem
8. voir dire
9. road kill
10. matricide
14. deathbed
15. doa

funny bone: what does a cannibal say before dinner?

b o n e
a p p e t i t

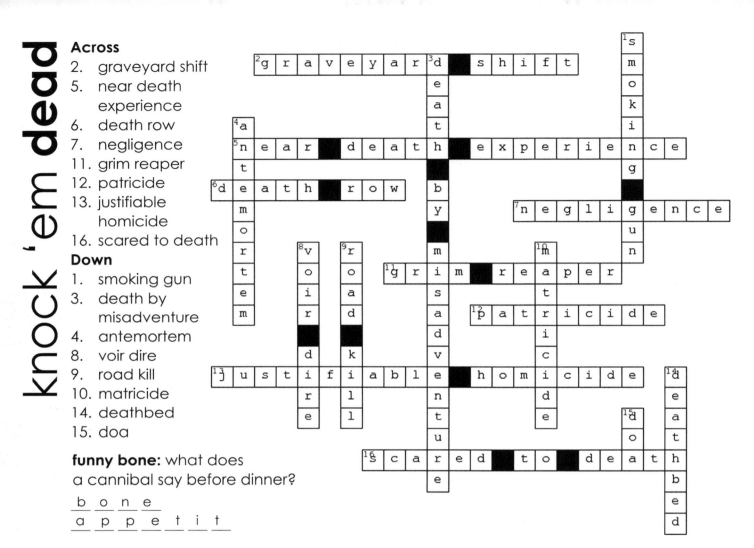

Transform the following words from one word to another in as few steps as possible.
Change only one letter at a time. For example, go from File to Bind: File, Mile, Mine, Mind, Bind.

crime	killer	prints	spatter
grave	bitten	faints	charged

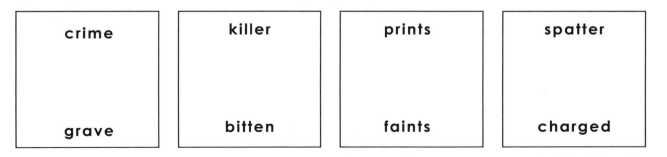

crime, grime, gripe, grape, grave. killer, kilter, filter, filler, bitter, bitten. prints, paints, points, faints. spatter, shatter, charter, charted, charged.

About the Author

The author lives in Ammon, Idaho with her long-suffering husband, Tyson, and their loyal dog, Lily.

Katy enjoys bacon, knitting, and the film How to Steal a Million.

She loves reading (especially scary stories), sometimes writing (mostly the procrastination of it), and occasionally even drawing.

She has amazing parents, three talented sisters, and a multi-lingual brother, who all put up with her crippling inability to make a decision.

This is her second coloring book.

Connect with me on social media at: @whatkatydrew on Instagram and Facebook.

Check out my blog to see more about the making of this book and other projects at www.whatkatydrew.blogspot.com.

Thank you, Diana. Without you, nothing would ever get done. <3

Tamam Shud